mis Fanton

A MICHAEL NEUGEBAUER BOOK

Text and photographs copyright © 1992 by Michio Hoshino.
First published in Switzerland under the title DAS BÄREN-KINDER-BUCH by Michael Neugebauer Verlag AG, Gossau Zurich, Switzerland.
English translation copyright © 1993 by North-South Books Inc.
The Animal Family series is supervised by biologist Sybille Kalas.
All rights reserved. No part of this book may be reproduced or utilized in any form or by any means, electronic or mechanical, including photocopying, recording, or any information storage and retrieval system, without permission in writing from the publisher.
First published in the United States and Canada in 1994 by North-South Books, an imprint of Nord-Süd Verlag AG, Gossau Zürich, Switzerland.
First published in Great Britain, Australia, and New Zealand in 1993 by Picture Book Studio Ltd., London. Reprinted in 1994 by North-South Books.
First paperback edition published in 1997.
Distributed in the United States by North-South Books Inc., New York.
Library of Congress Cataloging-in-Publication Data
Hoshino, Michio, 1952-
[Bären-Kinder-Buch. English]
The grizzly bear family book / Michio Hoshino ; translated by Karen Colligan-Taylor.
(The Animal family series)
"A Michael Neugebauer book"
1. Grizzly bear—Alaska—Juvenile literature. 2. Natural history—Alaska—Outdoor books—Juvenile literature. I. Title. II. Series.
QL737.C27H673 1993 599.74'446—dc20 92-36648

A CIP catalogue record for this book is available from The British Library.

ISBN 1-55858-350-5 (trade binding) 10 9 8 7 6 5 4 3 2 1
ISBN 1-55858-351-3 (library binding) 10 9 8 7 6 5 4 3 2
ISBN 1-55858-701-2 (paperback) 10 9 8 7 6 5 4 3 2 1
Printed in Belgium

For more information about our books, and the authors and artists
who create them, visit our web site: http://www.northsouth.com

Ask your bookseller for these other North-South Animal Family books:
THE CROCODILE FAMILY BOOK
THE DESERT FOX FAMILY BOOK
THE ELEPHANT FAMILY BOOK
THE LION FAMILY BOOK
THE PENGUIN FAMILY BOOK
THE POLAR BEAR FAMILY BOOK
THE WILD HORSE FAMILY BOOK

Michio Hoshino **The Grizzly Bear Family Book**

Translated by Karen Colligan-Taylor

NORTH-SOUTH BOOKS / NEW YORK / LONDON

Imagine meeting a grizzly bear in the wild. Not at the zoo, not in a book, but out in the open—a chance encounter with the real thing. Just you and the bear, face to face.

It happened to me once, when I was camping near Mount McKinley in Alaska. For more than half of each year, I hike through the mountains and plains of Alaska, the Great Land, with my tent on my back, taking pictures of the land which has attracted me since my teens.

Around four o'clock one morning I was awakened by something brushing against my tent. Wondering what it was, I rubbed my eyes and opened the tent flap. There, right in front of me, was a bear's face. I was startled, but the bear must have been even more surprised. It took one look at me and clumped hastily away.

I had never before been so close to a bear. And I knew then that I wanted to use my camera to record one year in the lives of the Alaskan grizzlies.

In midwinter the temperature here may fall to fifty degrees below zero. During this harsh time, a grizzly bear will sleep in a snug underground den, the entrance covered by a blanket of snow.

While the mother bear sleeps, her tiny cubs are born. They nurse and snuggle next to her until longer days and warmer temperatures signal the arrival of spring.

One day in April, as I hiked through the mountains called the Alaska Range, I noticed fresh bear tracks on the snowy slope. Following them with my binoculars, I spotted a mother bear and her cub walking through the snow.

The cold, biting wind was already giving way to spring breezes. When the bears come out of their dens, it's a sure sign that the long winter is over.

As the snow melts and shrinks into patches of crusty ice, wildflowers push their faces towards the sky. In the far north, the flowers are very small. But each blossom possesses tremendous strength. I am moved when I come upon these tiny shapes, living their lives to the fullest extent.

In early spring, grizzly bears also enjoy life to its fullest. Once I watched as a mother and her cub played tag on a slope across from me. The mother chased her cub across the grassy hillside. When she caught the youngster, she took it in her arms and hugged it to her gently, and they began to roll down the slope together. They seemed to be having such a wonderful time, I couldn't help but burst out laughing.

A nursing bear will often lie on her back and offer milk to her cub. If she has two, she will cradle one in each arm. I'm not sure that nursing tires her out, but afterwards the mother often spread-eagles on the ground, sound asleep.

People have such fearful images of bears. But is the affection and care of a human mother for her children so different from the love and tenderness the mother bear shows her cubs?

Grizzlies just emerging from their winter dens are as thin as they will be all year. They have not eaten for months, and in the snow-covered landscape, their first meal may be the carcass of a moose or caribou that did not survive

the winter. Near the sea, bears may find a beached whale, or a dead sea lion or walrus.

After the snow melts and the earth turns green, bears begin to eat roots and grasses. Sedges—grasses that grow in wetlands—are particularly important, because they grow rapidly in the early spring and are rich in protein.

Arctic ground squirrels are a popular food for bears, but it takes real work to catch one. An 850-pound bear chasing a 2-pound squirrel is a truly comical sight. When the squirrel dives into its hole, the bear begins digging

furiously with its front paws. But there may be many holes, all connected underground. Sometimes the squirrel will pop out of a hole behind the bear and watch it dig away.

Of course, many squirrels do get caught and eaten by bears. Scientists at Denali National Park in Alaska found that each grizzly bear eats about 400 ground squirrels a year.

Caribou, wolves, Dall sheep, moose, and many other animals give birth in the spring. They must keep constant watch over their newborns to protect them from danger.

One June afternoon I was sitting on a mountain slope looking down at a moose with her two young calves. For some reason the moose was uneasy, her ears pulled far back to the sides. A bear suddenly appeared from the bushes and rushed towards the calves.

The moose turned to confront the powerful bear. The bear stopped and the two faced off, staring at each other intently. A moment later the moose charged. The startled bear took off, with the moose close behind.

The moose had risked her life to protect her calves. And the bear retreated rather than risk being injured by the slashing hooves of the determined cow.

The bear will try again, of course, and next time it may be successful. But I have come to understand that when a bear catches a moose calf, it is not a sad event. The bear may have cubs of her own who will share in the meal. There will be new moose calves and new bear cubs next year, and life in the wilderness will go on. In nature, all living things, including humans, depend on other lives for their existence.

As summer nears, the daylight hours lengthen quickly until the nights are completely gone.

Imagine having no night at all. The sun moves around the sky in a big circle, always staying just above the horizon. Without a watch, it's hard to know when one day ends and the next begins. You may forget what day of the week it is, and even what month. And all the while, the sun's energy feeds the trees, grasses, and shrubs of the Alaskan wilderness.

In June salmon swim upstream in Alaska's rivers and streams, and bears are drawn to choice fishing spots. Grizzlies avoid contact with other bears during most of the year, but fishing season brings them shoulder to shoulder along the streams. With food temporarily abundant, they seem to tolerate one another more, but first a dominance order—an understanding of who bosses whom—must be established.

The stronger, more aggressive bears, usually males, command the best places. When a new bear joins a group, a brief struggle for dominance is often the result. Bears avoid fighting if at all possible, but two bears of nearly equal strength may wage a fierce battle. When two bears who have already fought meet again, the loser will automatically give up its place to the victor, avoiding another fight.

Bears use body language to express dominance or subservience within the temporary community at the river. By observing bears as they fish, I have learned some useful clues about the safest way to behave around bears in the wild.

One time I watched a mother bear with one cub, and another mother with two cubs, approach a river. While the mothers fished for salmon in the river, the cubs waited on the riverbank. Curiosity drew all three cubs together.

Suddenly the mother of the two cubs rushed up the bank. Would she kill the stranger? But the mother bear simply sniffed the cub that was not her own. Then the mother of the single cub realized what was happening, and charged out of the water to defend her young. Again it seemed as if there might be trouble. The cubs looked on nervously, staying near their mothers. In the end, the two families parted peacefully. Mother bears are usually quite tolerant of the cubs of others, even to the point of adopting strays and orphans.

I was surprised the first time I saw a bear catch a salmon, hold it briefly as if examining it, and then release it in the river. When salmon are rare, grizzlies will hungrily devour every one they catch. But at the height of the salmon

season, a bear may capture ten salmon an hour and can afford to be selective. Sometimes bears eat just the head and eggs, discarding the rest. The uneaten portion of the fish doesn't go to waste, however, because gulls swarm nearby, ready to grab the leftovers.

When a bear catches a salmon with its paws and mouth, it can probably smell the difference between a male fish and a female fish. The bear I saw

catching and releasing salmon may have been selecting only the female fish with their delicious eggs.

First-year cubs wait on the riverbank for their mothers to bring freshly caught salmon. By their second year, cubs wade in to fish for themselves. Although rarely successful at first, they learn by watching and imitating their mothers.

With the end of the salmon run, the bears' temporary society breaks up, each bear returning to its own mountain territory, where autumn food sources are now maturing.

The bugling of sandhill cranes
sweeping south in great ragged Vs
announces autumn across Alaska.
The animals of the Arctic grow lovely,
thick winter coats. Moose and caribou
antlers are now very large. Aspen and
birch forests turn golden, and the
tundra blazes red.

Blueberry, cranberry, and crowberry bushes blanket the ground, offering a rich harvest for bears.

"Don't bump heads with a bear when you go blueberry picking!" This frequently heard advice is no joke in Alaska. Both humans and bears become so engrossed in berry picking that they scarcely take a moment to lift their heads and look around. While you probably won't actually bump heads with a bear, it's wise to check your surroundings now and then.

Bears seem to like soapberries best of all. Wondering how they taste, I picked a ripe red one and popped it in my mouth. It didn't taste very good to me, but then I don't like fish heads, either.

It's wonderful to observe a huge bear holding a thin soapberry branch, gently stripping it of the delicate fruit.

As the days shorten, bears must put on a large store of fat to take them through winter. Berries are high in sugar, and the autumn feast can be critical to a bear's survival. With their shiny coats rippling as they move across the tundra, grizzlies consume an enormous amount of berries.

How many berries would you guess a grizzly can eat in one day? The bears in Denali National Park eat berries for twenty hours a day in late summer, hardly stopping to sleep. One bear may consume 200,000 berries in a single day! Bear droppings at this time of year consist mainly of partially digested berries. From the seeds in these droppings new bushes will grow to feed a new generation of bears.

One autumn day as I was hiking through the Brooks Range near the Arctic Circle, I suddenly noticed two bears running towards me from a riverbank. Were they coming at me on purpose, or did they not realize I was there? They appeared to be siblings, just old enough to leave their mother's care, but already powerful. Closer and closer they came, loping gracefully. My heart beat like a drum. When they were about twenty yards away, I raised my arms and shouted, *"Stop!"*

The two bears skidded to a halt as if in complete surprise. They stood up on their hind legs, wagging their heads from side to side, sniffing the air. I was so excited, I thought my heart would burst.

Then, as if they had finally become aware of my existence, they turned and raced off in the direction they'd come from. It had been a pretty frightening experience for me, but it must have been equally startling for the bears.

That night I couldn't fall asleep. The two grizzlies might be close by. Very few bears are interested in pursuing people, but still I felt somewhat uneasy. Unable to sleep, I thought about bears, about people, and about Alaska.

If there wasn't a single bear in all of Alaska, I could hike through the mountains with complete peace of mind. I could camp without worry. But what a dull place Alaska would be!

Here people share the land with bears. There is a certain wariness between people and bears. And that wariness forces upon us a valuable sense of humility.

People continue to tame and subjugate nature. But when we visit the few remaining scraps of wilderness where bears roam free, we can still feel an instinctive fear. How precious that feeling is. And how precious these places, and these bears, are.

Trophy hunters from the lower United States and from Europe come to Alaska to shoot grizzlies. They smile for the camera and stand, gun in hand, over the body of a dead bear. They hang their trophy on the wall—the head of a bear with its fangs bared, as if it was killed while attacking the heroic hunter. In truth, a high-powered rifle was fired from a great distance at a bear that was peacefully eating berries.

Just imagine: You're alone and unarmed on the arctic plain with a bear. You and the bear feel the same breeze pass over your faces. You—a human being—are on an equal footing with the bear.

How wonderful that would be. No matter how many books you read, no matter how much television you watch, there is no substitute for experiencing nature firsthand. If you cannot meet a bear in the wild, then you must try to imagine it—for even if you only imagine it, the feeling can be real. And it is the feeling that is important.

Today's snowfall marks the advent of winter. The daylight hours are shorter now. The aurora dances in the clear night sky. A mother bear and her half-grown cubs trace footprints in the new snow as they climb up the mountain to their den. The cubs will spend the long winter with their mother snug beneath the snow.

The snow continues to fall, and finally the tracks are gone. Alaska, the Great Land, settles down for a quiet winter sleep.